A book
is a present you can open
again and again.

·

THIS BOOK BELONGS TO

FROM

In the Jungle

Written by Fay Robinson

Illustrated by Paul Lopez

TREASURE TREE ™

World Book, Inc.
a Scott Fetzer company
Chicago   London   Sydney   Toronto

Printed in the United States of America
ISBN 0-7166-1623-8
Library of Congress Catalog Card No. 91-65746

8 9 10 11 12 13 14 15 99 98 97 96

Cover design by Rosa Cabrera
Book design by Lucy Smith

Imagine thick, green, tangled bushes and vines as far as you can see. Trees tower over you. All you see are plants, but above you hear the cries and roars and shrieks of many creatures. Want to explore? Let's step inside the wall of vines.

Where are you? You're in a jungle! Jungles are warm, rainy forests. Millions of curious creatures live here. High in the treetops, some of them swing from the branches and vines or quietly gaze. If you walk along and look carefully, here are some of the animals you may find.

Army ants march across the jungle floor. Sometimes they eat whatever is in their path. The tarantula, a giant spider, can be as large as your hand. And the Hercules beetle can be as big as a baseball!

The jungle is home to animals that eat insects, too. The anteater uses its long snout to sniff out ants and other bugs. It digs into their homes with its hooklike claws, then picks them up with its sticky tongue.

Did you know that wild guinea pigs live in the jungle? Their largest cousin, the capybara, lives there too. This huge guinea pig swims in the ponds and swampy areas of the jungle. A grown capybara can weigh as much as an adult person.

The largest animal in many jungles is the jaguar. Jaguars creep around in the lower branches of trees, ready to pounce on animals below. Some jaguars have black spots on their yellow and brown fur. Other jaguars are all black. The jaguar is a cat. It is at home in the water and swims well in the jungle rivers.

So many snakes live in the jungle. They slither along everywhere. See the tree boa in the lower branch? This snake is waiting for birds and other small animals it catches as prey.

The largest snake in the
world, a giant anaconda, swims
in the jungle rivers. It can grow
to be longer than a school bus.
When an animal comes to drink,
it may be caught by the
anaconda. The anaconda coils
around its catch, squeezes it,
and swallows it whole.

Birds in a rainbow of colors fly through the jungle sky. Parrots and parakeets are colorful and noisy birds that can't be missed. The toucan is also an eye-catcher. Its large bill looks like someone splashed paint on it. One kind of toucan is nicknamed "banana bill." Can you guess why? Toucans pick fruit with their bills, throw it backward in the air, catch, and swallow.

If you could climb the trees, you'd see
animals that almost never come to the
ground. One of the strangest is the sloth. At
first glance, you might think that sloths are
growing on the tree! These shaggy animals

spend most of their time hanging upside
down. They hang from the branches with
hooklike claws. They sleep much of the
time, and move so slowly that they can
take days to travel from tree to tree.

High in the branches, you'd also see frogs gripping the stems and leaves. Some tree frogs spend their whole lives above the ground. They have sticky pads on their feet that work like suction cups to help them climb around without falling.

The green iguana is at home in the treetops,
where it can bask in the sun. Look at the
iguana's sharp toenails. They help it grip the
branches. The iguana usually eats fruits and
leaves, as well as birds and insects. Perhaps
when this iguana is done resting it will eat.

Many different kinds of monkeys live in the trees. The monkey you might notice first is the howler monkey because its call is so loud. A shaggy mane covers its huge throat and voice box. Every morning and evening, the howler monkey opens its mouth in an *O* and roars. It will even howl at airplanes, people, and thunder.

The spider monkey gets its name from
its long thin arms, legs, and tail. It uses its
tail like an arm to grab and hold branches.
These monkeys move very fast, swinging
arm over arm through the trees. Sometimes

they run to the end of a branch and leap
through the air with their arms outstretched
to catch the next branch. They aren't always
on the go. These monkeys enjoy resting too.

Suppose you could look down at the jungle treetops from above. You'd see butterflies fluttering about, like splattering paint. A dazzling blue morpho butterfly rests on a leaf. It is at the jungle canopy. The canopy, like an umbrella, protects all the amazing creatures of the jungle.

How many
jungle animals
can you name?

More About Jungles

Scientists call jungles tropical rain forests. These forests are warm year-round, and rain falls in abundance. The broadleaf trees grow so close together that they prevent a lot of sunlight from filtering into the forest. As a result, only plants that do not need much sunlight can grow on the forest floor. Other plants— orchids, lichens, and vines—grow high on the trees where they can get the sunlight they need.

About half of all the different kinds of plants and animals in the world live in tropical rain forests.

There are three chief tropical rain forest regions in the world, mainly near the equator: in Africa, in Asia, and in the Americas (extending from Central America into much of South America). The animals in this book live in the rain forests of Central and South America.

Great areas of rain forest have been destroyed for lumber and for farming. The more we know about rain forests, the better we will be able to protect them.

To Parents

Children delight in hearing and reading about jungle creatures. *In the Jungle* will provide your child with interesting information about a number of these, as well as a bridge into learning some important concepts. Here are a few easy and natural ways your child can express feelings and understandings about the jungle animals in the book. You know your child and can best judge which ideas he or she will enjoy most.

Place stuffed animals about the house and invite your child to go with you on a "jungle safari." Push your way through the jungle. Look for animals high in "trees" and low on the "ground." "Listen" for animal sounds and imitate what you "hear."

Children love to decorate their names. In large, widely spaced letters, print your child's name on a piece of paper. Together, make each letter into an animal face by adding eyes, whiskers, nose, mouth, ears, and fur, for example.

Children can learn many things about animals by watching them. Ask your child where birds, rabbits, squirrels, or other animals might live nearby. Encourage your child to tell you what she or he has already noticed about the animals. Then visit the place to see what new things you can learn by watching. Make sure to talk about how the animals are alike or different from the jungle animals in this book.

Encourage your child and a friend to make a jungle scene. They can tear strips of colored paper to make trees and then paste the trees on a wrapping-paper background, using yarn or string to make vines. Encourage the children to draw favorite jungle animals in the background.

Your child may enjoy saying this rhyme with you, naming an animal and ending with appropriate sounds and actions. You can repeat the rhyme as many times as you wish, using different animal names.

I went to the jungle, and what did I see?
A great big —— looking right at me!
I looked at it; it looked back, too.
Here's what that —— can say and do!